# SAN ANTONIO
## *classic*
# DESSERTS

## HELEN THOMPSON
## & JANICE SHAY

*Photography by Robert Peacock*

**PELICAN PUBLISHING COMPANY**
Gretna 2011

Edited by Sarah Jones
Index by Sara LeVere

ISBN-9781455614585

Layout based on a design by Kit Wohl

Printed in China

Published by Pelican Publishing Company, Inc.
1000 Burmaster Street, Gretna, Louisiana 70053

# CONTENTS

## CUSTARDS, FLANS, SOUFFLES, & TORTES

## COBBLERS, PIES, & TARTS

## EMPANADAS, SOPAPILLAS, & CREPES

## CAKES, COOKIES, & PAN DULCE

## CANDIES, ICE CREAM, & ICES

## INDEX

# FOREWORD  *by Janice Shay*

I moved from Texas two decades ago, so when I recently returned to San Antonio I didn't expect it to be the same. It wasn't, it was better. Much better. And after a bit of thought, I realized that one of the main reasons this city has steadily improved with age is that it always respectfully keeps an eye on its past, while charging full speed ahead to the future.

No one who has ever seen or read about San Antonio's glorious 175-year-old history can fail to recognize the enduring Mexican influence in this beautiful city. It bears the visual stamp of its Spanish heritage in the lovely missions and architecture; and it is no surprise that you find these influences in restaurant menus, both old and new.

Of course, there are other influences that formed Texas cuisine—pioneers, cattle drives, and immigrants from Germany, Ireland, and other distant lands all brought their favorite sweets to this culture.

We offer the best of San Antonio's classic desserts in this book—cakes, cookies, pies, candy, custards, and more. You will also find desserts that feature some of Texas' best produce—Ruby Red grapefruit, pecans, and sweet potatoes, to name a few.

In order to help readers navigate their way through the Spanish names and ingredients in many of the recipes, we have included a glossary of terms for you, the reader.

## glossary

**CONCHAS**—*The Spanish word for "shells," often with scalloped edges; used to decorate traditional sweet bread rolls*

**PAN**—*The Spanish word for "bread," both sweet and savory*

**TORTILLA**—*A thin round of unleavened cornmeal; or wheat flour bread, usually eaten with a hot topping or filling*

**CAJETA SAUCE**—*Traditionally made with goat's milk, this rich, caramel-like sauce is a staple in Mexican kitchens*

**SOPAPILLA** (or Sopaipilla)—*A light, fluffy fried dough that can be served aloneor with sweet or savory fillings and accompaniments*

**FLAN**—*A popular Mexican dessert of sweetened egg custard with a caramel topping that can be served plain or flavored with fruit or cheese*

**TRES LECHES**—*Literally meaning "three milks," a sponge cake soaked in milk, sweetened condensed milk, and evaporated milk popular in Mexico and Central America*

**CHURROS**—*Fried-dough snacks, often shaped like a baton, and sometimes made from potato dough that originated in Spain; also sometimes called "Spanish doughnuts"*

**EMPANADA**—*Spanish or Portuguese stuffed bread or pastry that can be baked or fried; originating from the verb "empanar," meaning to wrap or coat in bread*

**PRALINE**—*A traditional Mexican cookie-sized candy made from sugar syrup, butter, and pecans*

**AGUA FRESCA**—*Literally means "fresh water," a sweet drink often served in summer months; made with water and crushed fruit*

**TEMBLEQUE**— *A dessert pudding made with coconut milk; it earns the Spanish word for "trembling" due to its gel-like texture*

**TORTE**—*A rich, dense dessert made with many eggs and little or no flour*

**SABAYON**—*A sweet, foamy, custard-like dessert served hot or chilled*

*Wall murals at Mi Tierra Café y Panadería celebrate not only the employees of the restaurant, but Mexican heroes, movie stars, and politicians.*

# INTRODUCTION    *by Helen Thompson*

San Antonio is one of the rare U.S. cities (New Orleans is one; Key West and Santa Fe might be the only others) where you can go and not be sure if you are in this country. Although San Antonio is the second largest city in Texas, it manages to be as sophisticated as a big city and display the steamy allure of the tropics at the same time. It's exotic, and exudes sensuality. But we're not the first to figure that out: Frederick Law Olmstead, the great architect of New York's Central Park, commented on this rare achievement in his 1857 book, *A Journey Through Texas*. "We have no city except perhaps New Orleans," he wrote, "that can vie, in point of the picturesque interest that attaches to odd and antiquated foreignness, with San Antonio." He elaborated, noting that the city had a "jumble of races, costumes, languages, and buildings."

So, when it comes to writing a book about desserts that most typify the city, you know you're in for a wild ride. The dominant culinary influence is Spanish—and that owes to the fact that the first residents arrived in 1731 from the Canary Islands, the Spanish archipelago off the northwest coast of Africa. When Mexico wrested its independence from Spain in 1821, Mexican Texas was part of the new nation. But the French had their influence here too, while they occupied nearby colonial Louisiana (which included a big chunk of what is now Texas). In the mid-1800s Germans were the largest immigrant group in Central Texas. And then, of course, Texas was a republic all on its own. Such demographic heave-ho might have been politically confusing, but it also means that the food here is really interesting.

Drama is par for the course, which made doing the research for this book a dizzying experience. First, we had to figure out the many recipes we wanted to include from San Antonio's zesty array of restaurants, eateries, and caterers. From that selection, we narrowed the list down further to target desserts that are the classic dishes of both the restaurant and the city. There are some icons included: Mi Tierra's luscious Pecan Pralines and La Fogata's Homemade Coconut Flan have secured their places in the city's culinary pantheon. There are others—like Biga on the Banks' Warm Sticky Toffee Pudding and Azuca Nuevo Latino's Pineapple Tembleque—that are destined for stardom.

These desserts are remarkable, not just because they are delicious, but also because they are distinctive. They represent a singular mindset that values authenticity and individuality, and are the result of many hours (and sometimes years) of tweaking and crafting. So, it's all the more remarkable that the chefs who created these desserts and made them famous so readily and generously agreed to share them with you, our reader, happily knowing that the act of creating good food can be one of those great shared experiences that only gets better the more you do it. I hope that these dessert recipes inspire home cooks to experiment and indulge, and to think sweet thoughts about the chefs who have given their best to this book.

# CUSTARDS, FLANS, SOUFFLES, & TORTES

Custard-based sweets are the starting point for many of our best desserts, and there's a reason why. It's the diplomat of desserts, suavely accommodating to palettes used to saucy French ingredients, to practical English adaptations, or to caramel-based Spanish versions. The custard or pudding probably came to Texas in the mess kits of French, Spanish, and English settlers—and in San Antonio, those cultures met head-on, with a little help from the Germans who were fond of zapping their puddings with port or brandy.

Not all custards are sweet or powerful, though. Relished for its subtlety, flan is probably the best-known Mexican dessert. It's a legacy of the Spanish, who descended—pastry-making skills, milk, and eggs in tow—on Mexico. Indigenous cooks combined these new ingredients with staples such as coconut (for a delicious example, try La Fogata's Coconut Flan), chocolate, fruits, and nuts, with seductive results.

*Biga on the Banks sets the standard for fine dining on the historic San Antonio Riverwalk, serving up gourmet dishes as bright and colorful as the seasons. Biga offers unparalleled outdoor dining, allowing for a breathtaking view of the river between bites of their award-winning desserts.*

# BIGA ON THE BANKS
# WARM STICKY TOFFEE PUDDING

## SERVES 6

**CUSTARD SAUCE**
2/3 cup whole milk
1/2 vanilla bean, split in half lengthwise, seeds removed and saved
4 large egg yolks
2 tablespoons granulated sugar
Pinch salt
1 teaspoon honey

**PUDDING**
5 tablespoons unsalted butter, softened, plus more for greasing ramekins
1/2 pound whole pitted dates, cut into 1/4-inch slices
3/4 teaspoon baking soda
2/3 cup boiling water

1 cup unbleached all-purpose flour
1/2 teaspoon baking powder
1/8 teaspoon salt
1/4 cup dark brown sugar
1/3 cup molasses
3/4 teaspoon vanilla extract
1 large egg

**TOFFEE SAUCE**
2 1/3 tablespoons unsalted butter
1/3 cup light brown sugar
3 tablespoons heavy cream
Pinch salt

**GARNISH**
Fresh strawberries, sliced

To prepare the custard sauce, bring the milk, vanilla seeds, and pod to a simmer in a medium saucepan over medium-high heat. When the milk begins to simmer, reduce the heat to low. In a medium bowl, whisk together the yolks, granulated sugar, and salt. Whisk 3 tablespoons of the hot milk mixture into the yolk mixture to temper it. Slowly whisk the tempered egg yolk into the simmering hot milk, and continue to whisk constantly for 2 minutes, or until the sauce is thick and coats the back of a spoon. Using a fine-mesh strainer, strain the mixture into a clean bowl, and stir in the honey. Cover with plastic wrap and refrigerate (or freeze to use later).

To make the pudding, preheat the oven to 325 degrees F. Grease six 4-ounce ramekins with butter and line the bottoms with small rounds of parchment paper. Arrange the ramekins in a small roasting pan.

Combine the dates, baking soda, and 2/3 cup boiling water in a medium bowl and set aside.

Whisk together the flour, baking powder, and salt in a small bowl. In the bowl of a standing mixer fitted with the paddle attachment, beat the remaining 5 tablespoons butter and dark brown sugar together on medium-low speed until just mixed, about 1 minute. Add the molasses and vanilla and beat until just combined. Scrape down the paddle and bowl using a rubber spatula. Continue mixing on medium low speed, add the egg, and beat until just combined. Add the date mixture and continue mixing until combined, then slowly add the flour mixture until just combined.

Divide the batter evenly among the ramekins. Fill the roasting pan with enough boiling water to reach halfway up the sides of the ramekins, making sure not to splash it into the puddings. Cover the pan tightly with foil, crimping the edges to seal. Bake for 35 minutes, or until the puddings are

slightly puffed and a butter knife inserted into the center of the puddings comes out clean.

To make the toffee sauce, melt the butter in a medium saucepan over medium heat. Whisk in the light brown sugar and cook, whisking occasionally, until the mixture reaches 250 degrees F. Do not let the mixture reach a simmer. Then, slowly whisk in the cream and salt and bring to a simmer. Remove the saucepan from the heat and transfer the sauce to a glass measuring cup. Cover tightly with plastic wrap to keep warm.

To serve, transfer the hot puddings to a wire rack to cool slightly. Run a paring knife around the edges of the ramekins to loosen. Pour the cold custard sauce, as desired, into each of six shallow bowls. Overturn the ramekins, releasing the puddings into the bowls. Pour the warm toffee sauce over the top of each pudding. Garnish with sliced strawberries and serve immediately.

# ROSARIO'S MEXICAN CAFÉ Y CANTINA
# RICE PUDDING

## SERVES 6 TO 8

*Opened in 1992 by Lisa Wong, Rosario's Mexican Café y Cantina has won numerous awards in the last 19 years. Praised by local publications including the* San Antonio Current *and the* San Antonio Express-News, *Rosario's boasts a young, loud, and fun-filled atmosphere that has become its trademark. This lively cantina also offers live music and a unique Latino art collection.* San Antonio Express-News *readers and critics alike have been raving about Roasrio's menu, voting it the "Best Mexican Restaurant" in 2009. Lisa has also been chosen for several "Entrepreneur of the Year" awards, and the restaurant has been recognized by* Zagat, Texas Monthly, *and* Hispanic Magazine, *among others.*

### BRANDY-SOAKED GOLDEN RAISINS
2 cups golden raisins
2/3 cups brandy

### CAJETA SAUCE
1 (14-ounce) can condensed milk
1 teaspoon vanilla extract
2 tablespoons half-and-half

### CANDIED ALMONDS
2 cups sliced almonds
1 2/3 cups white sugar
2 teaspoons ground cinnamon

### PUDDING
1 1/2 cups long-grain white rice
7 cups water
1 (4-inch) cinnamon stick
4 tablespoons white sugar
1 (12-ounce) can evaporated milk
1 (14-ounce) can condensed milk
1 1/2 cups heavy cream

### BUNUELOS
1/2 cup sugar
2 teaspoons ground cinnamon
1 package flour tortillas, cut into quarters
2 quarts vegetable oil, for frying

To prepare the raisins, soak the golden raisins in brandy overnight in a small, covered bowl.

To make the cajeta sauce, remove the label from the condensed milk can and place the entire can in a large pot of water (do not open the can). Allow the water to simmer just below the boiling point for at least 5 hours. Remove the pot from the heat and allow the can to cool while still in the pot. After it has cooled, open the can and pour the liquid into a bowl, or wide-mouthed jar. Add 1 teaspoon of vanilla extract and 2 tablespoons of half-and-half and stir well.

To prepare the candied almonds, toast the almonds on medium-high heat in a large, non-stick skillet, stirring constantly with a wooden spoon until the almonds are golden. Reduce the heat to medium and add 1 cup of the sugar and all the cinnamon, and continue to stir for 1 to 1 1/2 minutes, or until the sugar has melted. Mix in the remainder of the sugar and spread the almonds out onto a cookie sheet to cool.

To make the pudding, rinse the rice using a small mesh strainer. Stir the water, rice, cinnamon stick, and sugar in a medium-size heavy saucepan over medium-high heat. Bring the mixture to a boil and cook, uncovered, until the rice is tender, about 25 minutes. Stir in the evaporated milk, condensed milk, and heavy cream, then reduce the heat to low, and cook uncovered, stirring constantly, for 15 minutes, or until the mixture thickens. Remove from the heat and transfer to serving bowls.

To prepare the bunuelos, combine the sugar and cinnamon in a bowl and set aside. Heat oil to 350 degrees F in a pot with high sides (to prevent the oil from boiling over while frying). Using a slotted spoon, add tortillas to the oil and fry for approximately 1 1/2 minutes, or until golden brown. Remove from the oil, and drain on paper towels. Dip the tortillas into the prepared sugar. Dust off the excess sugar and place the bunuelos on a cookie sheet to cool.

To serve, spoon the pudding into a bowl or cup and top with 2 tablespoons of raisins. Drizzle cajeta sauce over each serving, and top with 2 bunuelos and 1 heaping tablespoon of candied almonds.

# THE FIG TREE
# BANANA CREME BRULEE

## SERVES 8

**BRULEE**
1 quart heavy cream
2 ounces banana liqueur
1 vanilla bean, split and scraped
12 egg yolks
1 cup sugar, plus more to dust over brulees
2 bananas, sliced

**GARNISH**
Whipped cream
Mint

Preheat the oven to 300 degrees F.

To make the brulee, bring the cream, banana liqueur, and vanilla bean to a boil in a saucepot over medium-high heat. Whisk the yolks and sugar in a glass mixing bowl and slowly pour the cream and vanilla into the yolks while continuing to whisk the mixture. Strain the mixture and pour into 1/2-inch-high brulee dishes.

Place the brulee dishes in a medium-size baking pan and pour enough water into the baking pan to reach halfway up the sides of the dishes. Bake at 300 degrees F for 30 minutes. The brulees are done when the custard has a gelatin-like texture. Check the doneness by tapping the brulee dishes to see if they have set.

Remove the brulees from the oven, allow them to cool, and transfer them to the refrigerator for at least 1 hour. When the brulees are completely set, sprinkle a thin layer of sugar over each creme brulee and caramalize the sugar using a kitchen torch. Spread the banana slices on a sheet pan and coat the slices with granulated sugar. Caramalize the sugar with a kitchen torch and place the sliced bananas on top of each of the custards. Top the brulee with a spoonful of whipped cream and a sprig of mint.

NOTE: Chef Bergeron recommends that you purchase a small propane blow torch for caramelizing the brulee. He says they are cheaper and easier to use than the kitchen version.

*Historically referred to as the Gray-Guilbeau House, The Fig Tree was the last private home in the La Villita historic arts village when the Phelps family purchased it as their personal residence in 1970. With so much history (and lots of public interest) surrounding the home, the Phelpses opened the home to the public on March 17, 1971. Located next door to its sister restaurant The Little Rhein Steakhouse, The Fig Tree has received several awards, including the esteemed DiRona membership every year since 1998, the AAA Four Diamond Award, and the Wine Spectator Award of Excellence. Expect to be completely enchanted by this historical home-turned-restaurant.*

# La Fogata
# Abuela's Coconut Flan

### SERVES 12

SYRUP
3 cups sugar
4 ounces water

FLAN
1 can Pet evaporated milk
1 can sweetened condensed milk
1/2 pint milk
6 eggs
1 teaspoon vanilla
½ pound coconut shavings

GARNISH
Chopped almonds
Cantaloupe, sliced

To make the syrup, pour the sugar into a saucepan over medium heat and cook, stirring frequently, for 10 minutes, or until the sugar has liquefied. When the sugar has liquefied, add the water slowly, stirring continuously, until the syrup turns a golden-brown color. Pour the syrup into the bottom of a 9-inch flan pan or medium-size bundt pan. Reserve 3 tablespoons of the syrup for garnish.

To prepare the flan, mix all the ingredients in a bowl using a hand mixer or wire whisk. Pour the mixture into the flan mold lined with the syrup. Place the flan mold into a small roasting pan and pour hot water into the roasting pan to reach halfway up the sides of the flan mold. Place the roasting pan into a 275-degree F oven, and bake for 1 hour and 45 minutes. Remove from the oven, take the flan mold from the roasting pan, cover, and allow it to cool in the refrigerator overnight.

To serve, place a chilled plate topside down onto the flan mold. Invert the flan onto the plate and carefully lift off the mold. Garnish with chopped almonds and slices of cantaloupe, and pour a little of the remaining syrup into each bowl.

*A northern Mexican favorite for San Antonians, La Fogata offers tasty Mexican treats in a beautifully designed, well-groomed hacienda environment, complete with a covered outdoor patio that provides the perfect al fresco dining experience in all types of weather. Acclaimed by regional publications like* Texas Monthly *as the ideal place to beat the heat of San Antonio's seasons, La Fogata serves up delicious fare in a relaxed setting.*

*Welcoming staff, colorful flags, and verdant gardens enhance the comfortable neighborhood-friendly atmosphere that is suggested by the restaurant's name—which literally means "the bonfire" in Spanish. This restaurant is truly an oasis just north of the historic city.*

## ALDACO'S
# FLAN DE VAINILLA

### SERVES 8

**CARAMEL**
1 cup sugar

**FLAN**
4 eggs
1 (12-ounce) can evaporated milk
1 cup whole milk
1 (14-ounce) can La Lechera condensed milk
1 1/2 tablespoons vanilla

**GARNISH**
2 teaspoons cinnamon powder for dusting
Mint

Preheat the oven to 300 degrees F.

To make the caramel, pour the sugar into a warm saucepan over medium heat, and cook, stirring slowly, for 8 to 10 minutes, or until the sugar becomes a golden-colored caramel sauce. Pour 1 1/2 tablespoons of the caramelized sugar into each of eight 6-ounce ramekins and allow the sugar to cool.

To make the flan, combine the eggs, evaporated milk, whole milk, condensed milk, and vanilla in a mixer. Blend until smooth, about 1/2 minute. Evenly distribute this mixture among the ramekins. Place the prepared ramekins into a small roasting pan and fill the pan with enough hot water to reach halfway up the sides of the ramekins.

Bake for 1 1/2 hours at 300 degrees F. The flan will be done when a knife inserted into the middle comes out clean, and the center of the flan is still soft. Allow the flan to cool down in the roasting pan, then remove it and refrigerate, covered, overnight for the best taste and texture.

Before serving, carefully run a knife along the edge of the flan to release it. Place a chilled plate topside down onto each ramekin. Invert the custard onto the plate and carefully lift off the ramekin.

To serve, spoon leftover caramel over the flan, dust with cinnamon powder, and garnish with a sprig of mint.

*Blanca Aldaco, San Antonio's own "hostess with the mostest," not only will serve you some of San Antonio's most sought-after Mexican desserts, but she will teach you how to cook, too. Cooking classes have become just another aspect of the service at Aldaco's, which has received countless awards over the years, including being named one of the top 75 restaurants in Texas by* Texas Monthly, *and one of the Top 100 Arts & Entertainment venues by the* San Antonio Express-News. The New York Times *recognized Aldaco's as the 7 p.m. event on their itinerary for a "36 Hours in San Antonio" article in an April, 2010, feature. Described as "a fiesta on heels or wheels" by a catering client, Blanca Aldaco's energy and passion for Mexican cuisine developed during her Guadalajara upbringing and are reflected in her menu and the atmosphere in which it is served.*

# ROSARIO'S MEXICAN CAFÉ Y CANTINA
# MEXICAN CHOCOLATE FLAN

### SERVES 6 TO 8

**CARAMEL**
1 cup granulated sugar
1 tablespoon water

**FLAN**
1 cup half-and-half
2 cups heavy cream
4 1/2 ounces Mexican chocolate (preferably El Popular brand, found at Mexican food stores), finely chopped
8 ounces bittersweet Callebut chocolate, finely chopped

5 eggs
2 tablespoons vanilla extract
3 tablespoons Kahlua liqueur

**BERRY MIX**
2 cups frozen berry mix
1 cup frozen strawberries, with syrup
1/2 cup white sugar

**CANDIED ALMONDS**
2 cups sliced almonds
1 2/3 cups white sugar
2 teaspoons ground cinnamon

Preheat the oven to 325 degrees F.

To prepare the caramel, combine the sugar and water in a heavy saucepan over low to medium-low heat. Cook, stirring constantly for 6 to 10 minutes, or until the sugar dissolves and the mixture begins to simmer. Using the handle of the pan, gently tilt the pan off the heat and shake to distribute the color evenly as the sugar caramelizes, about 10 minutes. When the sugar reaches a uniform light amber color, immediately remove the caramel from heat and pour it into individual ramekins or custard dishes, coating the bottom evenly by tilting each dish. Set the ramekins aside and let them cool.

To make the flan, bring the half-and-half and heavy cream to a boil in a heavy-bottomed saucepan over medium-high heat. When the milk begins to boil, remove the saucepan from the heat. Whisk the chopped chocolate into the hot milk until the chocolate is fully incorporated. In a separate bowl, whisk together the eggs, vanilla, and Kahlua until the mixture becomes foamy. Slowly whisk the hot milk mixture into the egg mixture. Strain using a fine mesh strainer .

Pour the custard into the prepared ramekins and set them into a large baking pan. Carefully pour enough hot water into the baking pan to reach halfway up the sides of the ramekins. Cover the entire pan with aluminum foil, place the pan on the middle rack of the oven, and bake 45 minutes to 1 hour, or until the flan is set around the edges and the centers jiggle slightly when shaken. Begin checking the custards at 20 minutes and check regularly until they are done. Once the flan begins to set, remove the pan from the oven and leave the ramekins in the baking pan to cool. Once cool, remove the ramekins from the baking pan and refrigerate for at least 2 hours, or up to 2 days.

To make the berry mix, combine the forzen berry mix, strawberries with syrup, and the sugar together in a medium-size heavy saucepan over medium-low heat. Simmer for 35 minutes, stirring occasionally with a wooden spoon. The berries and sugar will form their own syrup. Remove from the heat and pour into a small bowl to cool. Serve the cooled berries over the flan.

To prepare the candied almonds, toast the almonds on medium high in a large, non-stick skillet, stirring constantly with a wooden spoon until the almonds are golden. Reduce the heat to medium and add 1 cup of the sugar and all the cinnamon, and continue to stir for 1 to 2 minutes, or until the sugar has melted. Mix in the remainder of the sugar and spread the almonds out on a cookie sheet to cool.

To unmold and serve the flan, carefully dip the bottom of each ramekin briefly into hot water, then wipe dry. Run a thin knife around the edge of each ramekin to loosen the custard. Place a chilled plate topside down onto each ramekin. Invert the custard onto the plate and carefully lift off the ramekin. Garnish with the berries and candied almonds.

# Azuca Nuevo Latino
# Pineapple Tembleque

## SERVES 4 TO 6

**TEMBLEQUE**
1 quart coconut milk
3/4 cup cornstarch
1 teaspoon vanilla extract
8 ounces sugar

**PIÑA COLADA SAUCE**
1 cup condensed milk
1 cup coconut cream
1/2 cup pineapple juice

3 ounces white rum
1 cup creme anglaise (see recipe, p.40)

**GARNISH**
Pineapple slices
3 tablespoons granulated sugar
6 ounces coconut flakes
1/2 teaspoon powdered cinnamon
Mint

To make the tembleque, combine the coconut milk, cornstarch, vanilla extract, and granulated sugar in a saucepan and stir well. Cook the mixture over medium-high heat, stirring, bring to boil and cook until the mixture thickens, about 5 minutes. Continue to simmer for 2 to 3 minutes, stirring constantly, then remove from the heat and pour into individual dessert cups or molds. Allow to cool, then refrigerate.

To make the sauce, combine all the ingredients in a metal bowl and whisk to incorporate. Refrigerate the sauce until ready to use.

When ready to serve, unmold the tembleques and place each on a plate.

Coat the pineapple slices thickly with sugar and grill the slices until the sugar browns, or use a kitchen torch to brown the sugar. To serve, place the pineapple slices beside the tembleque. Pour the sauce over the tembleque and sprinkle the plate with coconut flakes and powdered cinnamon. Garnish with a sprig of mint.

*When chef and owner Rene Fernandez opened Azuca Nuevo Latino, he was inspired by a desire to unite the cuisine, service and atmosphere of the Caribbean, and Central and Latin America, with all of their glamour and vitality, in one place. Glamour can be seen in the colorful plates and rich atmosphere, and vitality is in no short supply—particularly on the weekend, when you can take salsa classes and dance merengue until the cows come home. Azuca has received recognition from* Hispanic Magazine *as one of the top 50 Hispanic Restaurants in the United States, and was named one of the best 10 restaurants in San Antonio in 2004 and 2005 by the Concierge Association.*

# Coco Chocolate Lounge & Bistro
# The Addiction

## SERVES 8 to 10

**CHOCOLATE PASTRY CREAM**
4 egg yolks
1/4 cup sugar
2 1/4 tablespoons cornstarch
2 cups whole milk
7 ounces bittersweet chocolate (preferably 55% cacao)
1 1/2 ounces butter

**WHITE CHOCOLATE SABAYON**
1/4 cup sugar
5 egg yolks
3 1/2 ounces white chocolate
3 cups whipped cream

**GARNISH**
1 package Oreo cookies, crumbled
Valrhona Chocolate Pearls (available at Valrhona.com)
Fresh berries (optional)
Chocolate straws (available at gourmet food or candy stores)
Mango or raspberry coulis (available at gourmet food stores, or see recipe, p. 42)
White chocolate disc, optional (see recipe, p. 93)

*Set in a space almost as sumptuous as its desserts, Coco Chocolate Lounge & Bistro will rekindle your love affair with chocolate through a menu that features subtle uses of cocoa in its savory dishes or in its extensive, decadent dessert menu. Opened in 2008 by former Las Canarias Maitre d' and hospitality director extraordinaire, Philippe Placé, Coco has received accolades and rave reviews from* Texas Monthly, San Antonio Express-News, *and local TV station WOAI 4. It was also a Zagat-rated San Antonio restaurant in 2009 and 2010, and it has received two Readers' Choice Awards from the* Express-News. *The charming Mr. Placé and his pastry chef concoct a magical dessert experience with this signature dessert that will have you coming back for more.*

To prepare the pastry cream, place the yolks in a mixing bowl. In a a separate bowl, combine the sugar and cornstarch and blend well. Add the sugar mixture to the yolks and whisk until they double in volume. While whisking the yolk mixture, bring the milk to a boil in a saucepot over medium-high heat. Slowly temper the hot milk into the yolk mixture, adding the milk slowly so the eggs do not scramble. Using a rubber spatula, scrape the mixture back into the hot saucepot. Cook the mixture on medium-high heat and whisk continuously for 1 1/2 minutes, allowing the mixture to come to a boil. Remove from the heat and add the chocolate and butter. Whisk until blended. Pour the cream into a container and chill in the refrigerator for 1 hour.

To make the white chocolate sabayon, whisk the sugar and yolks in a double boiler over medium heat for 4 to 5 minutes, or until the mixture thickens and doubles in volume. Remove the mixture from the heat and allow it to cool to room temperature.

Stir the white chocolate into a double boiler over low heat until it has fully melted. Remove from the heat and add 1/3 of the whipped cream to the chocolate, whisking vigorously until smooth. Add the yolk mixture to the chocolate and gently fold the remaining whipped cream into the mixture until it becomes light and creamy. Refrigerate for 2 hours, or until the sabayon sets.

Crumble the Oreo cookies by hand, then pulse in a food processor until they form a fine crumb texture. Set aside.

To serve, pipe the chocolate pastry cream inside a small, deep serving bowl. Fill just the outer layer of the bowl, leaving a small well for the second filling. Pipe the white sabayon into the well, just enough to fill the bottom. Sprinkle the chocolate pearls over the sabayon. Continue to layer the sabayon and the pearls until the mixture is level with the outer layer. Both fillings should be level with one another. Lightly sprinkle the crushed cookies over the top. Garnish with a white chocolate disc, sliced berries, chocolate straws, and coulis.

# SANDBAR FISH HOUSE & MARKET
## STRAWBERRY SOUFFLE

### SERVES 4 to 6

**STRAWBERRY SOUFFLE**
1 tablespoon butter, for ramekins
4 tablespoons sugar, plus 2 tablespoons for dusting ramekins
8 egg whites
8 ounces strawberry puree

**GARNISH**
1/4 cup powdered sugar for dusting
6 tablespoons vanilla ice cream, or your favorite flavor
3 strawberries, halved

Butter six 4-ounce ceramic ramekins, then coat the insides with sugar and pour out all the excess.

To make the strawberry souffle, place the egg whites in a mixer and beat on high for 50 seconds, then add the sugar. Beat the egg whites until stiff peaks form. Gently fold in the strawberry puree using a plastic spatula.

Spoon the mixture into the buttered dishes, making sure that the souffle batter is stacked evenly to ensure that it rises properly. Bake at 350 degrees F for 10 minutes, or until golden brown. Dust each souffle with powdered sugar, garnish with a strawberry half, and serve with ice cream.

*James Beard Award-nominated chef and entrepreneur Andrew Weissman has brought several culinary delights to San Antonio over the years, including the acclaimed Le Reve, Big'z Burger Joint, and the maritime dining experience, The Sandbar Fish House & Market. The Sandbar was established in 2005 and previously resided on Pecan Street before moving into the historic Pearl Brewery Complex, where diners can find another Andrew Weissman creation, Il Sogno Osteria. This casual fine dining spot sparkles with blue and white accents, and has received recognition from* Texas Monthly, Food & Wine, *and* San Antonio Current. *Bolstered by chef Chris Carlson's expertise, dishes that play to Texans' tastes and highlight local ingredients, like the Strawberry Souffle, are sure to dazzle tastebuds.*

# THE FIG TREE
# CHOCOLATE TORTE
# WITH BERRY SALAD

## YIELDS 17 SMALL TORTES

TORTE
16 ounces dark chocolate, chopped
2 sticks butter
1/4 cup Amaretto
8 eggs
1/4 cup sugar
1 jar apricot or seedless raspberry jam

CHOCOLATE GANACHE
21 ounces dark chocolate, finely chopped
1 quart heavy cream

CAJETA CARAMEL
1 gallon goat's milk
10 cinnamon sticks
4 cups sugar
1/4 teaspoon baking soda

GARNISH
Raspberries, blueberries, strawberries, and
    blackberries
Mint

At one of San Antonio's most historic restaurants, diners can choose to enjoy The Fig Tree's fine dining menu on the villa-style terrace overlooking the historic Riverwalk, or in the more intimate dining room. Situated in La Villita, one of the oldest parts of the city that boasts interesting shops and art galleries, this is a perfect spot for a quiet, romantic meal at the end of a long day.

To make the torte, melt the chocolate and butter together in a double boiler over low heat. Stir in the Amaretto.

Using a mixer, whisk the eggs and slowly add the sugar. Continue whisking until the mixture triples in size. Remove the chocolate mixture from the heat, and fold it into the eggs slowly, being careful not to scramble the egg mixture.

Pour 1/2 inch of the torte batter into each of the silicone baking molds with individual wells (available at restaurant supply stores). Place the baking molds into a larger pan and fill the pan with enough water to reach halfway up the sides of the baking molds. Bake the tortes at 350 degrees F for 7 to 11 minutes. The tortes will be done when a toothpick inserted into the center of the cake comes out clean.

To make the ganache, place the chopped chocolate in a glass mixing bowl. Bring the cream to a boil and pour it over the chopped chocolate. Cover the bowl with plastic wrap and allow the mixture to sit for 10 minutes. Then stir until the chocolate has completely melted.

To make the cajeta caramel sauce, combine all the ingredients except the baking soda in a saucepot over medium heat and cook for 1 to 1 1/2 hours, or until the mixutre has reduced to 2 cups. Whisk in the baking soda. The mixture will foam up once the baking soda is added; continue whisking until the foam dies down. Cook the sauce for another 2 to 3 minutes, until the caramel thickens enough to coat a spoon. Place the caramel in an ice bath, then skim off the foam that forms at the top before serving.

To assemble and serve, unmold the tortes and stack two of the chocolate tortes with a layer of apricot or raspberry jam in between the tortes. While the ganache is still warm, pour it over the tortes and allow the ganache to cool. Serve with sliced berries and caramel sauce.

*Las Ramblas's decor offers a beautiful contemporary dining experience.*

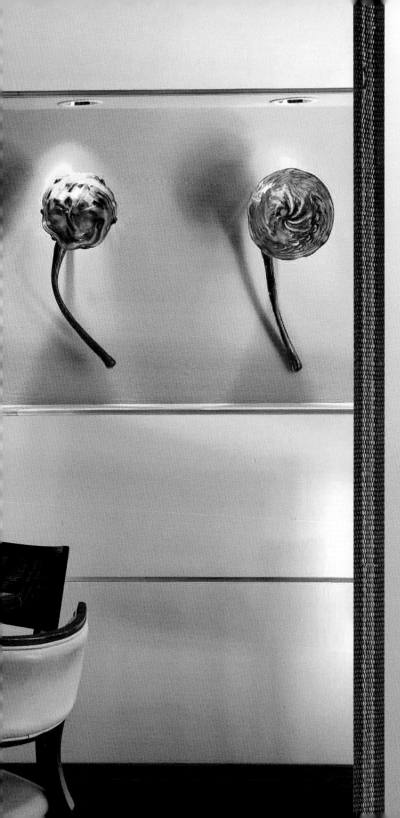

# COBBLERS, PIES, & TARTS

The cobbler is what happens when the concept of pie seems just too straight-laced for a casual dinner. Filled to capacity and beyond with fruit, cobblers are accessible—with gooey goodness bubbling out, unfettered by latticed strips of dough or a smothering canopy of crust. Cobblers are very Southern, but oh-so-adaptable, as demonstrated by the warm mango version that's a crowd-pleaser at Azuca Nuevo Latino.

But pie has its value, and one of the earliest advantages was its portability. In the Stone Age, honey was the treat wrapped inside a crust made of oats, wheat, or rye. These little pies were essential for long trips—especially if the journey was to the great beyond. Evidence found in the tomb of Rameses II suggests the pharaoh was fortified with a supply of crusty galettes as he was readied for his transition from an earthly life. For our money, Auden's Lemon Meringue Pie is a little piece of heaven on a plate.

The tart is an an elaborate version of pudding, ensconced in a pastry shell and often prettily decorated with seasonal fruit. Las Ramblas's Ruby Red Grapefruit Tart is a superb way to feature one of Texas' favorite fruits.

*The brainchild of San Antonio superstar chef Bruce Auden of Biga on the Banks, Auden's Kitchen opened in early 2010 and welcomed diners with open arms into its bustling kitchen. Serving up everyday fare with a refined touch in a casual yet sophisticated space, Auden's Kitchen is said to reflect the way Bruce cooks at home with seasonal dishes and daily specials. Traditional American cuisine is peppered with international favorites that have been crossing South Texans' plates for years. Eating your Lemon Meringue Pie or other house-made dessert at the chef's counter will give you a front-row seat to all the action as food is pulled from the wood-burning oven and dishes come flying out of the kitchen.*

# AUDEN'S KITCHEN
# LEMON MERINGUE PIE

## SERVES 6

### CRUST
1 1/3 cups, plus 1 tablespoon all-purpose flour
Pinch fine sea salt
5 ounces cream cheese
5 ounces unsalted butter

### FILLING
1/4 cup, plus 1 teaspoon cornstarch
1 1/3 cups granulated sugar
1/4 teaspoon fine sea salt
1/2 cup water
3 tablespoons butter

Zest of 1 lemon
1 cup lemon juice
8 egg yolks, gently beaten

### BROWN SUGAR MERINGUE
1/4 cup, plus 1 tablespoon cold water
1 tablespoon cornstarch
5 egg whites
Juice of 1/4 lemon
5 tablespoons, plus 1 teaspoon granulated sugar
1 tablespoon dark brown sugar

To make the crust, combine the flour and salt in the bowl of a mixer. Using the paddle attachment, add the cream cheese and briefly mix. Add the butter and mix until mostly combined. The dough should just come together with lumps the size of peas.

Lightly flour a work surface, knead the dough briefly, and smooth it into a disc. Lightly flour the dough on top and roll it out to a 1/8-inch thickness. Gently press the dough into a pie pan, crimping the edges. Place a layer of plastic wrap over the crust and fill to the top with dry beans or pie weights. Wrap the plastic back over the top of the beans, so that the edges of the pie dough are exposed. Bake at 325 degrees F for 20 minutes, or until the crust is just turning golden brown. Remove the beans and plastic, and continue baking for 6 to 8 minutes, or until the bottom dough turns golden, too. Cool on a wire rack.

To make the filling, combine all the ingredients except the yolks in a saucepot over medium heat. Allow the mixture to simmer just until steam begins to rise from the liquid. Remove the mixture from the heat and add the yolks slowly, whisking constantly. Return to heat, bring the mixture to a boil, and cook for 2 minutes, stirring constantly. Pour the filling into the baked pie crust. Cover the surface with plastic wrap that touches the filling and set aside to cool.

To prepare the meringue, combine the water and cornstarch in a small saucepot over medium heat. Bring to a boil, stirring continuously, until the mixture becomes thick and translucent. Do not boil more than 2 minutes. Remove from the heat and place the pot in an ice bath until the mixture comes to room temperature.

In the bowl of an electric mixer fitted with the whisk attachment, whisk the egg whites on medium speed until foamy, then add the lemon juice. Whisk on high until the meringue forms soft peaks, then gradually add both sugars with the mixer running. Beat until stiff peaks form. The whites should be very thick and gathering inside the whisk. Add the cornstarch mixture to the meringue, and mix on high for 1 to 2 minutes, or until the meringue is smooth and thick. Spread over the cooled lemon filling with a spatula. Make sure the meringue touches the crust all the way around, sealing in the lemon filling. Be careful not to work the meringue too much, or it will start to deflate. Bake at 350 degrees F for 15 to 20 minutes, or until the peaks and edges are lightly browned.

# LAS RAMBLAS AT HOTEL CONTESSA
# RUBY RED GRAPEFRUIT TART

SERVES 4

FILLING
5 1/3 cups sweetened condensed milk
1/2 cup lime juice
1 cup Ruby Red grapefruit juice

CRUST
4 (4-inch) tart shells
1/2 cup butter
2 cups graham cracker crumbs

CREME ANGLAISE (see recipe, p. 40)

GARNISH
Grapefruit segments
Mint
Blueberries
Whipped Ccream

To make the filling, combine the sweetened condensed milk, lime juice, and grapefruit juice in a bowl and mix well.

To make the crust, put the butter and graham cracker crumbs in a separate bowl, and cut together. Press the cracker crumb mixture into the bottom of the buttered tart shells.

Pour the filling into the tart shells and bake in a 350-degree F oven for 15 minutes or until a toothpick inserted into the center comes out dry.

Pour enough creme anglaise to just cover the bottom of a shallow bowl. Garnish each tart with grapefruit segments, blueberries, whipped cream, and a sprig of mint.

*The famous Hotel Contessa's Four Diamond Resort restaurant Las Ramblas has taken its direction since 2009 from award-winning chef Brian West, who was invited to cook at the James Beard House Benchmark Holiday Dinner in December 2010. Chef West was also featured as a "Top Chef" in the January 2010 edition of* San Antonio Destinations. *Las Ramblas's menu echoes the Spanish influence of Texas' history, specializing in Old and New World tapas and Spanish and Mediterranean cuisine. The Ruby Red Grapefruit Tart highlights a classic Texas ingredient.*

# SANDBAR FISH HOUSE & MARKET
# SWEET POTATO PECAN PIE

## SERVES 8 to 10

**DOUGH**
2 cups all-purpose flour
4 tablespoons sugar
1/2 teaspoon salt
6 tablespoons butter, cold
4 tablespoons cold milk
1 egg

**FILLING**
3 to 4 sweet potatoes, cooked (about 2 cups)
1/2 cup lightly-packed brown sugar
4 tablespoons sugar
1 egg
2 tablespoons cream
2 tablespoons softened butter
2 tablespoons vanilla extract

1/2 teaspoon salt
1/2 teaspoon ground cinnamon
1/2 teaspoon ground nutmeg

**PIE SYRUP**
1 1/2 cups light corn syrup
1 1/2 cups sugar
4 small eggs
3 tablespoons butter, melted
4 tablespoons vanilla extract
Pinch salt
1 teaspoon cinnamon
2 tablespoons molasses
2 cups pecan halves

To prepare the dough, combine the flour, sugar, and salt. Using a fork, mix in the cold butter until the mixture resembles coarse sand. Add the milk and egg, mixing the dough until it forms a cohesive ball—be sure not to overmix. Flatten the dough into a 6-inch disc and refrigerate for at least an hour. Roll the dough out to fit a 9-inch pie pan and refrigerate for another hour.

To make the filling, roast the sweet potatoes in a 400 degree F oven for 40 to 60 minutes, or until they become soft. Remove the potatoes from the oven and allow them to cool. Peel and place them into a mixing bowl with the sugars, egg, cream, butter, vanilla, salt, cinnamon, and nutmeg, and whisk until the mixture forms a smooth puree. Set aside.

To make the syrup, combine the corn syrup, sugar, eggs, butter, vanilla, salt, cinnamon, and molasses. Mix to a smooth consistency. The sugar should be mostly dissolved.

To assemble the pie, fill the bottom third of the cooled pie shell with the sweet potato filling. Add the 2 cups of pecan halves, and pour the syrup over the top. Bake at 325 degrees F for 1 1/2 hours or until the topping has set. Allow to cool 1 hour and serve with whipped cream.

*Specializing in (you guessed it!) fine seafood-inspired cuisines, The Sandbar Fish House & Market attracts a young crowd, and the lively, bright cafe is a great stop for visitors to the Pearl Brewery Complex.*

*Established in 1881, the Pearl Brewing Company began to produce Pearl Beer in 1886. The site was named the San Antonio Brewing Company later, and through prohibition the brewery continued to concoct refreshing soda water, near-beer, and ice to stay afloat. The parent company purchased the Pabst Brewing Company and eventually, all production was transferred to Miller Brewing in Fort Worth. The Pearl Brewery closed in 2001, only to be revived a few years later as a shopping, dining, and entertainment destination at the northernmost navigable point of the San Antonio River. Now home to shops, businesses, and new restaurants run by cutting edge chefs, "the Pearl," as it is called, is as active as ever.*

# Azuca Nuevo Latino
# Fruit Gratin

## SERVES 4

### GRATIN
1/2 mango, peeled and sliced
1 kiwi, peeled and sliced
1/2 orange, peeled and sliced
1/2 apple, peeled and sliced
1/2 banana, peeled and sliced
8 blackberries
10 blueberries
1 strawberry, sliced
1 slice pineapple
1 slice papaya
4 ounces creme anglaise
2 ounces granulated sugar

### CREME ANGLAISE
1 cup heavy cream
2 teaspoons vanilla extract
4 egg yolks
1/3 cup granulated sugar
1 tablespoon rum

*When you enter this casual, fun "new Latin" restaurant you are struck by the energetic space with its explosion of color and art. The walls are bedecked with colorful paintings and sculptural glass pieces reminiscent of exotic flowers. It is a perfect setting for the food, which is as colorful and spicy as the atmosphere.*

To make the creme anglaise, heat the cream and vanilla in a small, heavy saucepan over medium heat, until the mixture begins to boil. In a metal bowl, beat the egg yolks and sugar together. Temper the egg yolk mixture by pouring 1/2 cup of the hot cream mixture very slowly into the bowl of yolks, beating constantly. Add the tempered egg yolk mixture back into the saucepan with the remaining cream, whisking constantly. Beat in the rum. Continue cooking over low heat, stirring constantly, until the mixture thickens enough to coat the back of spoon. Refrigerate the mixture until ready to use.

On a large flat plate, spread the creme anglaise and arrange the fruit over top decoratively. Sprinkle granulated sugar over the entire plate. Using a kitchen torch, brown the sugar and cream and serve.

# Azuca Nuevo Latino
# Mango Cobbler

## SERVES 4 to 6

**COBBLER**
2 pounds fresh mangos, peeled and cut
8 ounces granulated sugar, plus 1 teaspoon
for sprinkling
1 (10 x 20-inch sheet size) package puff pastry
1 egg white

**CREME CHANTILLY**
1 cup heavy whipping cream
1 tablespoon powdered sugar

**MANGO COULIS**
2 fresh or frozen mangos, peeled and sliced
1 cup granulated sugar
Juice of 1/2 lime

**RASPBERRY COULIS**
2 cups fresh or frozen raspberries
1 cup granulated sugar
Juice of 1/2 lime

**GARNISH**
1 fresh mango, sliced
1 fried crisp garnish (see Bunuelo recipe, p. 16)
1 rosette creme chantilly (see recipe below)
2 ounces mango coulis (see recipe below)
2 ounces raspberry coulis
Mint
Strawberries, halved
Powdered sugar, for dusting

To make the cobbler, combine the mangos with the granulated sugar in a medium saucepan and simmer over medium heat for 10 minutes, or until the mixture becomes syrupy. Allow the mixture to cool.

Place half a sheet of puff pastry, a 10 x 10-inch sheet, into the bottom of a baking pan and bake at 350 degrees F for 9 minutes.

Spoon the cooled mango mixture on top of the pre-cooked pastry and cover with the other half of the pastry sheet. Brush the top of the pastry dough with an egg wash (egg white mixed with a splash of water) and sprinkle with the remaining sugar. Return to the oven and cook for 25 to 30 minutes, or until the pastry is golden brown on the top. Remove from the oven and refrigerate overnight.

To prepare the creme chantilly, pour the heavy whipping cream in a metal bowl, and place the metal bowl over an ice bath. With a thin whisk, whip the cream until you achieve soft peaks. Add the powdered sugar and continue whisking until stiff peaks form. Refrigerate until ready to use.

To make the raspberry coulis, heat the raspberries, sugar, and lime juice in a saucepan over medium-high heat. Cook until the sugar dissolves, stirring constantly with a wooden spoon. Simmer for 5 minutes, then remove from heat and allow to cool. Puree the mixture in a blender and refrigerate until ready to use.

To make the mango coulis, combine the mango pieces, sugar, and lime juice in a small saucepan over medium-high heat. Simmer until the mangos are soft. Refrigerate until ready to use.

To serve, heat the cobbler in a 350-degree F oven for 8 to 10 minutes, or until the center is warm. Place the warm cobbler in a shallow bowl and decorate with a fried crisp, creme chantilly, mango and raspberry coulis, fresh berries, and a sprig of mint. Dust with powdered sugar and serve warm.

*Texas has, no doubt, seen its fair share of cobblers —most often the peach, apple, plum, cherry or berry variety. The origins of cobblers have been traced back to the American West in the mid-1800s. American settlers brought the tradition of English puddings with them to the frontier, but pioneer cooks seldom had proper ovens to cook these dishes. Out of necessity the cobbler was born, with its adaptable fillings (canned, fresh or dried fruit could be used) and its biscuit-like crust that was perfect for baking in a cowboy's Dutch oven. Chef Rene Fernandez brings Caribbean and Latin flavors to this classic dessert with the mangos.*

*Nights on the Riverwalk are always fun-filled, and offer an array of dining choices.*

# EMPANADAS, SOPAPILLAS, & CREPES

We are the beneficiaries of one of Mexico's greatest gifts to dessert-lovers everywhere: many of the treats traditionally delegated to the end of the meal have morphed into foods that are consumed during the meal, or as accompaniments. Some, like the empanada—a dough-wrapped pastry stuffed with meats, vegetables, or fruits—are all-purpose foods that adapt to any occasion. At Los Barrios, fruit fillings such as guava or apple are popular, and might even remind Anglophiles of a type of Cornish pastie favored by the British. The French had their own interpretation. The crepe folds over its filling, allowing diners to sneak a peak, where they might find—as in the case of Ernesto's Cajeta Crepes—something sweet and comforting.

In the case of sopapillas—a lighter fried version of the empanada—the puffed hollow at the center is mostly hot air, proof that sometimes air is the most delicious filling of all. Meant to be drizzled in honey, sopapillas are one of those utilitarian accompaniments that are routinely served at meals and easy to take for granted. That is, until you get a version—such as Aldaco's light-as-air rendition—that reminds you how great the simple things in life can be.

# LOS BARRIOS
# EMPANADAS DE MANZANA

## YIELDS 10 EMPANADAS

FILLING
3 firm baking apples (such as Granny Smith)
1 cup granulated sugar
1 teaspoon ground cinnamon
1/2 teaspoon ground nutmeg

PASTRY
3 cups all-purpose flour
1 1/2 teaspoons baking powder
Pinch salt
1/2 cup vegetable shortening
3/4 cup water
1/4 cup powdered sugar, for dusting

To prepare the filling, peel and core the apples and slice thinly. Place the apples, sugar, cinnamon and nutmeg in a saucepan over medium heat. Cook for 10 to 12 minutes, stirring constantly, until the apples are soft. Remove from the heat and refrigerate to cool.

To make the pastry, combine the flour, baking powder, and salt in a large bowl. Add the shortening and mix until a course meal forms. Add the water and mix until well blended. Divide the dough into 10 pieces, and shape into dough balls, each the size of a golfball.

Preheat the oven to 325 degrees F. On a floured surface, using a floured rolling pin, roll out each ball of dough into a 4-inch round. Put 1 to 2 tablespoons of the fruit filling in the center and fold the dough over to make a half-moon-shaped turnover. Pinch the edges of the dough together to seal. Arrange the empanadas on a greased baking sheet and bake 12 to 15 minutes, or until golden brown. Sprinkle with powdered sugar and serve warm.

NOTE: You can deep-fry the empanadas rather than bake them if you prefer. Fry in batches in 2 quarts of hot oil, until golden brown, about 1 1/2 minutes on each side. Different fruits can be used to make several varieties of filling.

*When it first opened in 1979, Los Barrios was operating out of a small boat garage in San Antonio. After outgrowing that location in six short months, Viola Barrios moved her operation to an old Dairy Queen just north of downtown. While this family-run business has graduated from the Dairy Queen location, not much else has changed about the way they do things. Viola's daughter Diana and her siblings Teresa and Louis honor their mother's legacy by continuing to serve the same delicious family-style Mexican cuisine that Viola did more than 30 years ago. The Barrios "casero-style" cooking has drawn attention from the likes of Food Network's Bobby Flay (Diana beat Bobby in a puffy taco "Throwdown" in 2007); the White House in June 2010, where Diana was invited to cook at the Congressional Picnic; and Good Morning America with Emeril Lagasse. Diana's empanadas are not to be missed.*

# ERNESTO'S RESTAURANT
# CAJETA CREPES

## YIELDS 8 CREPES

CREPES
1 3/4 cups flour
3/4 cup milk
3/4 cup water
4 eggs
1 teaspoon vanilla
1/2 stick butter, melted, plus butter for pan
Pinch salt

SAUCE
2 quarts whole milk
3 cups sugar
3/4 teaspoon baking soda
1 1/2 cups pecans, chopped
2 tablespoons butter
2 ounces brandy

*While Ernesto's Restaurant is located in a modest building on Jackson Keller, Ernesto and Grace Torres are anything but shy about sharing their passion for Mexican food. The proprietors of Ernesto's since 1979, they are quick to greet you and eager to make you feel right at home during your dining experience. After operating a restaurant for more than 30 years, Ernesto and Grace know how diners want to end a meal of classic Mexican food—these simple, tasty Cajeta Crepes with brandy sauce will satisfy your sweet tooth.*

To make the sauce, add the milk, sugar, and baking soda to a large saucepot and bring to a boil over medium-high heat. Simmer, stirring occasionally, for 4 to 5 hours, or until the sauce is very thick and caramel colored. Sauce may be refrigerated until ready for use.

To prepare the crepes, thoroughly mix the flour, milk, water, eggs, vanilla, melted butter, and salt until smooth. Let the batter stand for 1 to 2 hours, or refrigerate overnight.

To make the crepes, heat a dab of butter in a crepe pan over medium-low heat. Pour 1/4 cup of the batter on one corner of the pan then tilt the pan so the batter covers the entire surface. When the batter is no longer liquid, turn the crepe and lightly brown on both sides. Stack the crepes and cover until ready to use.

Saute the pecans in butter, then place them on a cookie sheet in a 350-degree F oven and toast for 8 minutes, or until crisp. Set aside.

When ready to serve, reheat 1 1/2 cups of the sauce in a 12- to 14-inch skillet along with the pecans and brandy. When the sauce simmers, add 1 crepe at a time, using tongs or 2 forks to fold into a triangular shape. When all are folded, remove from heat and transfer to serving dishes. Spoon additional sauce over each serving and garnish with the pecans.

Leftover cajeta sauce may be kept refrigerated for two weeks.

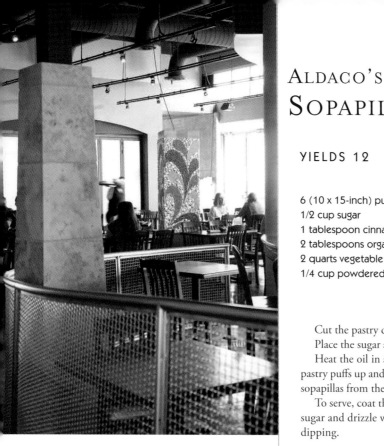

# ALDACO'S
# SOPAPILLAS

## YIELDS 12

6 (10 x 15-inch) puff pastry sheets, thawed
1/2 cup sugar
1 tablespoon cinnamon
2 tablespoons organic agave nectar, or honey
2 quarts vegetable oil
1/4 cup powdered sugar, for dusting

Cut the pastry dough into 3-inch squares or triangles.

Place the sugar and cinnamon in a plastic bag and shake to combine.

Heat the oil in a deep-fryer or heavy skillet to 375 degrees F. Fry the dough in hot oil until the pastry puffs up and turns golden brown, then turn and cook the other side until golden. Remove the sopapillas from the oil and drain on paper towels.

To serve, coat the sopapillas evenly with the sugar and cinnamon mixture. Dust with powdered sugar and drizzle with honey immediately before serving, or serve with agave nectar or honey for dipping.

*Blanca Aldaco opened the restaurant in 1989 at its original Commerce Street location, and before long the restaurant had moved to accommodate its customers and is now spread out over two locations: Aldaco's Stone Oak and Aldaco's at Historic Sunset Station.*

*Sopapillas are said to have originated about 200 years ago in Albuquerque, New Mexico. Often served with honey or syrup, this light pastry resembles an airy pillow and is sometimes filled with savory ingredients like refried beans. Aldaco's version is a crowd-pleaser, with a cinnamon-sugar dusted over the top.*

# LAS RAMBLAS AT HOTEL CONTESSA
# CHURROS

## YIELDS 15 CHURROS

### CHURROS
17 ounces water
1 teaspoon salt
2 1/2 cups, plus 1 tablespoon sifted flour
2 quarts canola oil for frying
Powdered sugar, for dusting

### CAJETA SAUCE
1 (14-ounce) can sweetened condensed milk
1 teaspoon pumpkin spice
2 teaspoons vanilla extract
Heavy cream, as needed

### CHOCOLATE SAUCE
1 cup sugar
1/3 cup cocoa
3 tablespoons cornstarch
1 cup water
2 teaspoons orange extract

### GARNISH
Strawberries, halved
Vanilla ice cream
Chocolate shavings

*Located on San Antonio's picturesque Riverwalk, Hotel Contessa offers a modern, luxurious dining experience in a Mediterranean-inspired setting. This contemporary, 12-story hotel manages to complement the style of historic San Antonio with its warm interiors and beautiful decor. The Las Ramblas dining room is no exception, offering exquisite dining in a relaxed yet striking atmosphere—what better place to enjoy Food & Beverage Director Shane Bruns' own churros recipe?*

To make the churros, bring the water and salt to a boil in a 3-quart, stainless steel saucepot, then lower the heat to medium, pour in all the flour, and mix with a wooden spatula until a consistent, even dough forms. Remove the dough from the heat and continue to knead the dough with the wooden spoon until the dough becomes smooth. When the dough is completely smooth, fill a churro maker, or a large pastry bag fitted with a large star tip so you can squeeze the dough through. Do not overfill the pastry bag.

Heat the oil to 375 degrees F in a large frying pan or small fryer, and drop in strips of dough that are about 3 inches long. Fry for 3 to 4 minutes, or until the churros are golden brown, turning the churros in the oil to ensure even browning. Remove the churros with a slotted spoon and drain them in a colander or on a paper towel.

To make the cajeta sauce, cover the entire unopened can of sweetened condensed milk with water in a medium saucepot. Allow the water to simmer for 2 hours. Remove the pot from the heat and allow it to cool. Once the can has cooled enough to touch, open the can and pour the sauce out into a mixing bowl and add the spice and vanilla extract. If the sauce is too thick, you can thin it out by whisking in heavy cream until the desired texture is achieved.

To make the chocolate sauce, combine all ingredients except the orange extract together in a saucepan. Over medium heat, stir the mixture continuously for 15 minutes, or until the sauce thickens. Remove the pan from the heat and add 2 teaspoons of orange extract. Allow the chocolate to cool.

To serve, drizzle the churros with chocolate and cajeta sauce and garnish with vanilla ice cream, chocolate shavings, and strawberry slices.

*The historic Guenther House museum and restaurant.*

# CAKES, COOKIES, & PAN DULCE

What's a party without a chocolate cake? When it comes to chocolate, we owe what might be considered a national addiction to the Aztecs, who were the first to grasp the allure of the seed of the tropical Theobroma cacao tree. Don't let Don Strange's Triple Chocolate Cake fool you by its simplicity, it is nothing short of decadent.

Even more universally enjoyed than cakes are cookies, as any child will attest. After all, you can eat them with your fingers and not feel guilty about overindulging! The tradition of serving cookies at special feasts, such as Panifico Bake Shop's tasty little Wedding Cookies, is a wonderful way to feature this simple dessert.

Definitely not for eating with your fingers, the tres leches cake is in a class by itself. Its origin is unclear, but it is reported to have come from a recipe on the back of evaporated milk or condensed milk cans sold in Latin America to promote the use of the product. Densely soaked in evaporated milk, sweetened condensed milk, and cream, and often topped with a cloud of whipped cream, the tres leches cake eventually takes on a pudding-like quality that transforms a bite of the sponge cake into a luscious mouthful. Acenar's Tres Leches Cake, which we chose for the cover of this book, leads the pack with their moist, tasty cake.

# ACENAR
# TRES LECHES CAKE

## SERVES 12

**CAKE**
3 cups all-purpose flour
1 1/2 tablespoons baking powder
3/4 cup whole milk
1 1/2 tablespoons vanilla extract
9 large eggs, separated
3 cups granulated sugar

**SOAKING LIQUID**
2 (12-ounce) cans evaporated milk
1 (14-ounce) can condensed milk
3 cups whole milk
1 1/2 cups cajeta quemada, plus more for
    garnish (sweetened caramelized milk,
    available in Mexican specialty stores)

**TOPPING & GARNISH**
6 to 8 cups whipped cream
6 strawberries, halved, or other seasonal fruit
Mint
1/4 cup powdered sugar, for dusting

Preheat the oven to 350 degrees F. Spray a 9 x 13-inch sheet pan with cooking spray and cover the bottom with parchment paper. Spray the parchment and sides of the pan with the cooking spray, too.

To make the cake, sift together the all-purpose flour and baking powder in a medium bowl. In a large cup, combine the milk and vanilla extract.

Using a mixer with the paddle attachment on medium speed, mix the egg whites with sugar until smooth. Add the egg yolks and scrape the bottom and sides of the bowl so no clumps of sugar remain. Beat the mixture until well blended, alternately adding the flour and milk, starting with 1 cup of flour and followed by half the milk. Once the last cup of flour is incorporated, scrape the bottom and sides again and beat until smooth and slightly thickened. Pour the batter into the prepared pan and bake for 25 to 30 minutes or until an inserted toothpick comes out clean.

While the cake is baking, make the soaking liquid. Combine the three types of milk with the cajeta, stirring until well blended. Refrigerate until ready to use.

While the cake is still slightly warm, but not hot, invert it onto a sheet pan, peel off the parchment and trim off the edges (this will enable better absorption of the liquid and give a neater appearance when serving). Return the cake to the baking pan so that the flat side is facing up. Using a toothpick, pick small holes throughout the surface of the cake and pour the milk mixture over the cake until the texture of the cake feels spongy to the touch. Cover and refrigerate overnight so that there are no internal dry spots. The next day, drain any excess milk and top with whipped cream. Chill until ready to serve.

Garnish each serving with powdered sugar, slices of seasonal fruit, a sprig of mint, and a drizzle of cajeta sauce.

*This Riverwalk restaurant and bar is all that it claims to be in its "Hot Mex, Cool Bar" tag line. With a fuchsia and gold color scheme, there is no doubt that the latest project of Rosario's owner and successful San Antonio entrepreneur, Lisa Wong, is the hottest new addition to San Antonio's famed dining corridor. With rave reviews about both Acenar's meals and its milieu from Texas Monthly, San Antonio Magazine, Zagat and 10best.com, their new twists on old Texas and Mexican regional foods are sure to please even the most modern of foodies. Acenar fulfills the needs of those with a love for originality and innovation just as gracefully as it satisfies those with a longing for traditional tastes.*

# BIN 555
# CABRALES BLUE CHEESE
# CHEESECAKE WITH BRANDIED
# CHERRIES

**SERVES 8 to 10**

CRUST
2 tablespoons sugar
2 cups graham cracker crumbs
5 ounces melted butter

CHEESECAKE
2 pounds cream cheese, softened
1/2 cup blue cheese
1 3/4 cups, plus 1 teaspoon sugar
6 tablespoons cornstarch

1 vanilla bean, split and scraped
5 eggs
2 egg yolks
Cream, as needed

BRANDIED CHERRIES
1 cup brandy
1/2 cup granulated sugar
2 cups dried cherries
Mint leaves, sliced into long, thin strips

To make the crust, mix the sugar, graham cracker crumbs, and butter. Line a spring-form pan with foil and parchment and press the crust mixture into a 1/8-inch thickness in the bottom of the pan.

Preheat the oven to 350 degrees F.

To make the cheesecake, cream together cheeses, sugar, and cornstarch in a mixer. As you mix, add the vanilla bean, split and scraped. Slowly add in the eggs and yolks until they are fully incorporated. Add cream to thin the mixture, if needed. Remove the vanilla beans and pour the mixture onto the crust in the spring-form pan. Place the pan into a small roasting pan and pour enough water into the roasting pan to reach halfway up the sides of the spring-form pan. Bake 1 1/2 hours, turning the cake every 30 minutes until the cheesecake is set.

To prepare the brandied cherries, prepare a simple syrup by dissolving granulated sugar in the brandy in a saucepan over medium-low heat. Add the cherries and simmer for 30 minutes over low heat until a syrupy texture is achieved. Spoon the brandied cherries and its syrup over the cheesecake, sprinkle with the mint strips, and serve.

*San Antonians looking for Mediterranean- and Spanish-inspired dishes search no further than the upscale yet relaxed dining room of Bin 555. Located on San Antonio's North Side in the Shops at Artisan Alley, Bin 555 offers up delicious dishes that are packed with flavor. Desserts such as their Cabrales Blue Cheese Cheesecake are hand-crafted by chef and owner Jason Dady, who has been recognized on the list of 40 Under 40 "Rising Stars" in the* San Antonio Business Journal, *and was chosen to cook at the James Beard House twice— in June 2005 and again in August 2009. Jason and his brother, Jake Dady, own and operate four other restaurants in the San Antonio area: Tre Trattoria, Two Bros. BBQ Market, Restaurant Insignia, and their flagship restaurant, The Lodge at Castle Hills.*

# WARM ALMOND BASQUE CAKE

## YIELDS 10 SMALL CAKES

**DOUGH**

2 cups sugar

2 cups flour

2 1/2 tablespoons ground almonds, plus
  more for garnish

2 teaspoons yeast

1/4 teaspoon salt

2 egg yolks

1/8 cup rum

10 tablespoons butter, softened

**CREAM**

1 1/2 cups milk

1/2 vanilla bean

3 egg yolks

1/2 cup sugar

1/4 cup flour

1 1/2 teaspoons rum

**GARNISH**

1 cup ground almonds

1 pint raspberries

10 scoops vanilla ice cream

To make the dough, combine the sugar, flour, almonds, yeast, and salt. Add the egg yolks, rum, and butter and mix by hand. Crumble the mixture until it forms a ball. Wrap the dough in plastic wrap and refrigerate for 4 hours.

To make the cream, heat the milk and vanilla bean in a saucepan over medium heat. In a medium bowl combine the egg yolks and sugar. Slowly add in the flour and rum. Add the milk mixture to the eggs and combine thoroughly. Strain the mixture and return it to the heat. Stir constantly until the mixture thickens. Refrigerate for 1 hour before serving.

Spray ten 4-ounce tins with pan spray. Divide the dough into 10 balls of equal size and roll out each ball of dough to 1/4-inch thickness. Fill each of the metal tin bottoms and sides with the dough. Put about 1 tablespoon of cream into each metal tin and top with 1/4 inch of pastry. Seal the sides and bake at 350 degrees F for 30 to 45 minutes.

Top each cake with a small scoop of vanilla ice cream, garnish with ground almonds and raspberries, and serve.

*The Basque Cake has a rustic origin, much removed from this more refined approach, and it traditionally featured a black cherry filling. Because the seasonal fruit is often hard to find, an almond-flavored custard filling has been substituted. Basque country is a region of the western Pyrenees that spans the border of France and Spain on the Atlantic coast, and influences from both of those countries can be found in much of their food—and in the menu at Bin 555.*

# LAS CANARIAS AT LA MANSION DEL RIO
# WARM LEMON CAKE WITH SWEET CORN MOUSSE

### SERVES 8 to 10

**LEMON CURD**
9 ounces butter
2 1/2 cups sugar
1 cup, plus 2 1/2 tablespoons lemon juice
7 eggs
2 egg yolks

**CAKE**
2 3/4 cups white chocolate chips
3 tablespoons milk
1/2 cup butter, plus 2 tablespoons for mold
1/8 cup condensed milk
9 eggs, lightly beaten
Zest of 3 lemons

1 1/2 cups all-purpose flour
1/3 cup rice flour
5 tablespoons polenta

**GARNISH**
Blackberries
Creme chantilly (see recipe, p. 42)

**SWEET CORN MOUSSE**
6 ears fresh corn
4 cups milk
12 egg yolks
1 cup sugar
2 cups heavy cream

*Located in the Omni Hotels La Mansion del Rio on San Antonio's Riverwalk, Las Canarias is marked by its intimate and relaxed atmosphere. The restaurant has received the prestigious AAA Four Diamond Award and was both San Antonio Express-News Readers' and Critics' Choice for Best Hotel Restaurant in 2009. Diners can choose to dine on the patio overlooking the riverwalk, or get lost in the comfort and grace of the Las Canarias dining room while devouring delicious treats like Warm Lemon Cake.*

To prepare the lemon curd, melt the butter in a saucepan. Add half of the sugar and the lemon juice and bring the mixture to a boil. Mix the eggs, yolks, and remaining sugar in a separate bowl and temper the lemon mixture, adding the egg mixture slowly and taking care not to scramble the eggs. Cook on low heat until the curd has thickened. Allow the mixture to cool, then portion into tablespoon-size balls and freeze until you are ready to use.

To make the cake, melt the white chocolate, milk, and butter in a bowl and whisk to combine. Add the condensed milk, followed by the eggs and lemon zest. Mix in the all-purpose flour, rice flour, and polenta.

Preheat the oven to 350 degrees F.

Grease individual molds with butter, then dust each mold lightly with sugar. Fill each mold 2/3 with cake batter. Drop a ball of frozen lemon curd into the center of each mold, then fill with the remaining cake batter (about 1/2 inch from the top of the mold). If you are planning to bake one cake rather than use individual serving molds, pour half the cake batter into a 9-inch cake pan, drop balls of the lemon curd over the surface of the batter, then pour the remaining batter over the curd. Bake for 10 to12 minutes.

To make the sweet corn mousse, heat the milk and corn in a saucepan over medium heat to bring out the corn's flavor. Once the milk begins to simmer, remove the corn. Temper the milk and corn mixture with yolks and sugar by adding the yolk mixture to the milk mixture slowly, being careful not to scramble the eggs. Cook over medium-low heat until the mixture has thickened slightly, then add the cream. Puree the mixture in a blender and strain. Churn in an ice cream bowl, or freeze until ready to use. Serve the cake with the mousse and garnish with creme chantilly and blackberries.

# THE GUENTHER HOUSE
# LEMON BARS

## YIELDS 2 DOZEN

### DOUGH
2 1/4 cups White Wings All Purpose Flour
2 sticks butter, softened
1/2 cup powdered sugar, plus more
  for sprinkling

### FILLING
2 cups granulated sugar
1/2 cup lemon juice
1/4 cup White Wings all purpose fFlour
4 large eggs
Zest of 1 lemon

Preheat the oven to 350 degrees F.

Spray a 9 x 13 x 2-inch baking pan with cooking spray.

To make the dough, combine the flour, butter, and powdered sugar in a large mixing bowl. Mix until a soft dough forms. Press the dough into the bottom of the prepared baking pan and bake for 20 to 25 minutes, or until it is lightly browned.

While the shell is baking, make the filling by beating together the sugar, lemon juice, flour, eggs, and lemon zest. Pour the filling over the hot crust, return the pan to the oven, and bake another 20 minutes, or until set.

Turn the bars out onto a wire rack to cool before cutting into 2-inch bars. Sift powdered sugar over the tops of the bars and serve.

*The restaurant at The Guenther House offers diners a bountiful breakfast, and lunch options ranging from soups and salads to sandwiches and enchiladas. Visitors may choose to dine outside in the lush greenery surrounding the restaurant or in one of the house's historic dining rooms.*

*The Guenther House has a rich and well-preserved history. Flour mill owner Guenther's family home, the museum now houses memorabilia from both the mill and the family, including antique baking accessories, cookie cutters, Dresden china plates, original flour bags, and other more personal items—like Erhard Guenther's silver-plated trophy from the Casino Club Bowling Team of 1897. Learning the history behind the house and its baking traditions makes this picturesque dining experience more fun.*

# Don Strange of Texas, Inc.
# Triple Chocolate Cake

## SERVES 8 to 10

CAKE
1 box Duncan Hines chocolate cake mix
1 small box instant chocolate pudding
2/3 cup sour cream
3 eggs
1 cup water
1/4 cup canola oil
4 cups semisweet chocolate chips
1/4 cup all-purpose flour

CHOCOLATE FUDGE ICING
4 tablespoons unsalted butter
1/4 cup milk
1 cup sugar
1 cup semisweet chocolate chips
1 cup chopped pecans, for topping

*Don Strange of Texas, Inc. catering has a history in Texas nearly as long as its list of prominent clientele. The company began as a small grocery store opened by Edith and Joe Strange in 1952. Two years later the couple purchased the restaurant next door, and the place became known as "The Party House, Inc." Thirty two years later, Edith and Joe's son Don had taken over, and the name was changed to Don Strange of Texas, Inc. The caterer's colorful business portfolio includes catering the Congressional BBQ on the South Lawn of the White House in 1990 at the request of President Bush. Don was awarded the "HOSPY" Award by San Antonio Hotel and Motel Association for Best Catering in San Antonio in 2001, before he passed away in 2010. The firm is now run by his eldest son Brian and his siblings, making certain that Don Strange's catering company continues to create succulent sweets like this Triple Chocolate Cake for San Antonians.*

To make the cake, combine all ingredients except the chocolate chips and flour in the bowl of a mixer and beat for 2 minutes. Grease and flour 2 (9-inch) loaf pans and set aside.

Toss the chocolate chips with the flour to coat, then transfer them to a wire strainer and shake off the excess flour. Add the chocolate chips to the cake batter and beat just until blended. Divide and pour the batter into the 2 prepared loaf pans and bake according to package instructions for the cake mix. Allow the layers to cool completely on wire racks.

To make the chocolate fudge icing, combine the butter, milk, and sugar in a heavy-bottomed, 2-quart saucepan over medium-high heat. Bring to a boil, stirring often, and cook for 1 minute, stirring constantly. Remove from the heat and whisk in the chocolate chips. Continue to whisk until the chips melt and the icing is smooth. Cool the icing for 10 to 15 minutes before frosting the cake.

To frost the cake, spread a layer of icing over the bottom layer, then stack the second layer on top and frost the rest of the cake on all sides. Sprinkle the top of the cake with the chopped pecans.

# LAS RAMBLAS AT HOTEL CONTESSA
## CAJETA GOAT CHEESECAKE

**SERVES 8 to 10**

**CHEESECAKE**
2 1/2 pounds cream cheese
1 pound goat cheese
1 3/4 cups sugar
6 tablespoons cornstarch
5 eggs
Zest of 1/2 orange
1/2 vanilla bean, scraped

**CRUST**
1/4 cup butter
1 cup graham cracker crumbs

**GARNISH**
1 orange, thinly sliced
Blueberries
10 strawberries, halved
1 tablespoon cajeta sauce (found in the Latin
    section of a grocery, or see recipe, p. 53)
Whipped cream
Mint

To make the cheesecake, use a mixer to cream together the cream cheese, goat cheese, sugar, and cornstarch. With the mixer still running, add 1 egg at a time, stopping to scrape the sides of the bowl. Mix in the orange zest and vanilla bean scrapings.

To prepare the crust, cut together the butter and graham cracker crumbs using a separate bowl. Press the graham cracker mixture into the bottom of a buttered cake pan.

Preheat the oven to 350 degrees F.

Pour the cheesecake batter into the cake pan and place into a roasting pan filled with enough water to reach halfway up the sides of the cake pan. Bake for 40 minutes, or until a toothpick inserted in the center comes out dry.

Garnish with slices of orange, fresh berries, cajeta sauce, whipped cream, and a sprig of mint.

*Beautiful interiors magnify the culinary delights that Las Ramblas has to offer. Warm golds and modern décor make the space as delightful as dishes such as this Cajeta Goat Cheesecake, created by pastry chef Suellen Golden.*

# THE GUENTHER HOUSE
# BERRY SHORTCAKE

## SERVES 8

### BERRY MIX
1 pint strawberries, sliced
1/2 pint raspberries
1/2 pint blackberries
1 1/4 cups sugar, divided

### SHORTCAKES
1 1/2 cups whipping cream
4 1/2 cups Pioneer Original Biscuit & Baking Mix
4 tablespoons butter at room temperature,
  cubed

### WHIPPED CREAM
2 cups whipping cream
1 cup powdered sugar, plus more for dusting
1/2 teaspoon almond extract
1/2 teaspoon vanilla extract

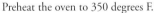

Preheat the oven to 350 degrees F.

Line a cookie sheet with parchment paper or spray the sheet with vegetable spray.

Mix the berries and 1 cup of sugar in a bowl and set aside.

To prepare the shortcakes, use a mixer with the paddle attachment and combine the whipping cream, the baking mix, butter, and 1/4 cup sugar. Mix just until the dough comes together. Be careful not to overmix.

Separate the shortcake dough into 8 equal parts, and arrange on the cookie sheet. Sprinkle sugar on top of each shortcake. Bake the cakes for 25 to 30 minutes. Remove them from the oven and allow them to cool completely.

To make the whipped cream, use a mixer fitted with the whisk attachment and whip 2 cups of cream on high speed until soft peaks form. Add the powdered sugar and extracts and mix well. Cover the cream and refrigerate until you are ready to serve.

To assemble the shortcakes, slice the cakes in half and place a scoop of the whipped cream on the bottom half, followed by a spoonful of fresh berries. Set the top half of the cake atop the berries and dust with powdered sugar before serving.

*C. H. Guenther & Son began as a family business that provided the highest quality flour to the community of Fredericksburg, Texas. In 1859, the enterprising C. H. Guenther sold his mill in Fredericksburg and bought a new one in San Antonio. One hundred and fifty years later, the Guenther House still reflects the miller's trade with accents of plaster corn and wheat bundles used in the décor. The Guenther House was built between 1915 and 1918 in the popular Art Nouveau style, and became a restaurant 25 years ago. Famous for its breakfast and baked goods, any visit to The Guenther House restaurant is not complete without a taste of its special Guenther House Berry Shortcake.*

# THE GUENTHER HOUSE
# CHERRY CREAM CHEESE PASTRY

### SERVES 9 TO 12

**DOUGH**
6 ounces cream cheese
1/3 cup butter, softened
3 1/3 cups Pioneer Biscuit & Baking Mix
1/2 cup milk

**FILLING**
8 ounces cream cheese, softened
1/3 cup sugar
1/8 teaspoon almond extract
1 (21-ounce) can cherry pie filling

**GLAZE**
1 cup powdered sugar, sifted
5 teaspoons milk
1/2 teaspoon vanilla

Preheat the oven to 350 degrees F.

To make the dough, blend the cream cheese and butter until the mixture is uniform and smooth. Add the baking mix and stir until the mixture resembles coarse crumbs. While mixing, add the milk in a slow, steady stream until a soft dough forms. Turn the dough out onto a lightly floured surface and knead it only 4 to 6 strokes, just enough to bring the dough together in a ball. Roll the dough out to an 11 x 17-inch rectangle, then cut to fit onto a cookie sheet. Cover and refrigerate while preparing the filling.

To prepare the filling, mix the cream cheese, sugar, and almond extract until it is well combined, uniform, and smooth. Spread the cheese filling lengthwise down the center of the dough in a 3-inch wide strip. Spoon the cherry pie filling over the cream cheese filling.

Cut 4 1/2 x 1-inch strips of dough, perpendicular to the filling along each side of the dough. Crisscross these strips to cover the filling, beginning at one end and working toward the other. Pinch and tuck dough ends under on both ends to seal.

Bake for 28 to 30 minutes, or until the pastry is golden brown. Cool the pastry on the cookie sheet.

To make the glaze, mix all the ingredients in a bowl until smooth, then drizzle the glaze over the cooled pastry and serve.

*A walk around the beautiful grounds of the Guenther House and the ajacent mill will reveal many antiques and memorabilia related to this German family who immigrated to Texas and built a successful mill and flour business. In the early- to mid-1800s, many German immigrants came to Texas in search of their fortune, and their traditions and tastes live on in central Texas.*

# PANIFICO BAKE SHOP
# CONCHAS (PAN DE HUEVO)

### YIELDS 22 CONCHAS

**CONCHAS**

3 teaspoons instant yeast
1/2 cup water, warm
1/2 cup evaporated milk
1/2 cup granulated sugar
6 tablespoons vegetable shortening, soft
2 teaspoons salt
1/2 cup eggs (about 3 eggs)
3 teaspoons Mexican vanilla (found in Latin section of grocery or specialty food shops)
3 1/4 cups, plus 2 tablespoons flour, divided
3 teaspoons coarsely ground cinnamon

**PASTE**

1 pound powdered sugar, sifted
1 pound vegetable shortening
1 pound bread flour
1/4 cup cocoa powder, as needed
1 small bottle yellow food coloring, as needed
1/2 cup very soft or melted shortening

*Panifico Bake Shop started out as a corner "panaderia" (Spanish for bakery) more than 40 years ago. When current owners Edna Miggins and her husband John bought it, she made it her priority to continue the tradition of running a friendly neighborhood bakery where folks drop by daily to buy their sweets and breads. With her classic pastry chef training, Miggins offers a large array of cookies, conchas, and other treats for every-one in the family, while ensuring that customers— most of whom she knows by name—feel at home in her shop. Edna offers both traditional Mexican pastries—like the ever popular egg bread Pan de Huevo—as well as more contemporary treats.*

Preheat the oven to 375 degrees F.

To make the conchas, use a mixer with the dough hook attachment and combine the yeast and warm water. Mix in the milk, sugar, vegetable shortening, salt, eggs, Mexican vanilla, and half of the flour. Gradually mix in the remaining flour and the cinnamon. At medium speed, knead until the dough is smooth and elastic.

Place the dough on a lightly floured surface, cover, and let it rise in a warm place until it has doubled in size, about 1 to 1 1/2 hours.

While the dough is resting, prepare the paste. Combine the sugar, shortening, and flour in a mixing bowl fitted with the paddle attachment. Beat the ingredients into a smooth paste. If different colors of paste are desired, divide the paste into 3 parts. For the chocolate paste, add enough cocoa powder to tint the topping to the desired shade. Do the same with the yellow food coloring for the yellow paste. Set aside.

Split the dough into 2-ounce pieces. Shape each piece into a round ball and place on a greased cookie sheet, with enough space to allow for rising. Brush each piece with very soft or melted short-ening.

Divide the paste into ½ -ounce portions. Pat a portion of the paste onto the top of the dough balls to create a small circle of paste over each piece of dough. If desired, use a knife to carve designs on the topping—the traditional clamshell design is where the name "conchas" is derived.

Cover and let the conchas rise until doubled in size, about 1 hour. Take care to not let the dough rise too much or the topping will spread out too much during baking. Bake for 15 minutes, or until the bottom of the dough is lightly browned. Serve warm or cold.

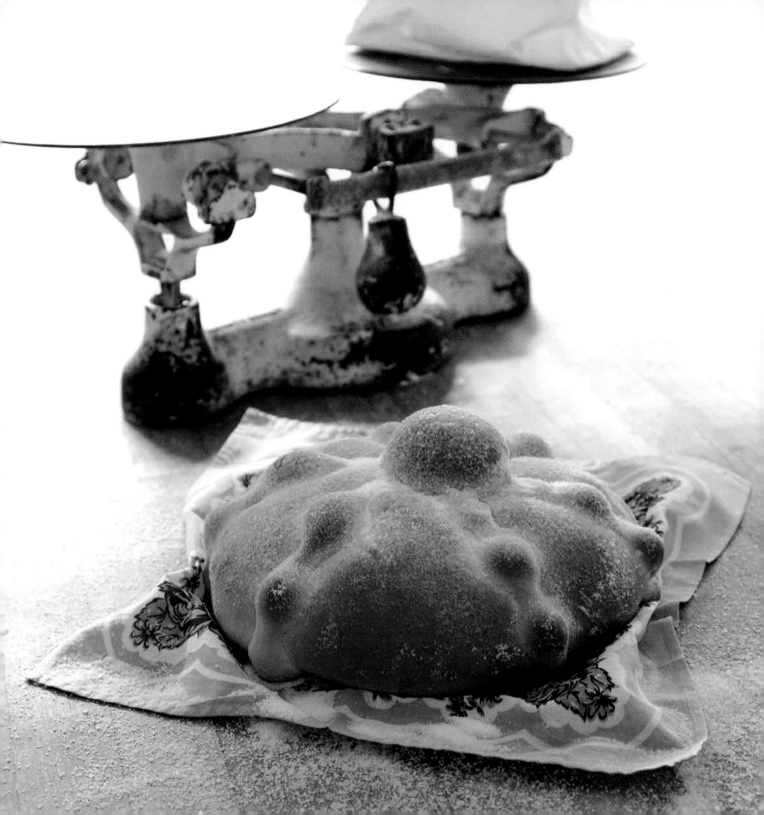

# PANIFICO BAKE SHOP
# PAN DE MUERTO

## YIELDS 2 LOAVES

1 tablespoon yeast
1/2 cup water
1/2 cup evaporated milk
1/2 cup granulated sugar
3 tablespoons vegetable shortening
2 1/4 teaspoons salt
3 eggs
1/2 tablespoon orange extract

2 1/4 teaspoons orange peel (be careful not to include the white, fleshy part of the peel)
3 2/3 cups bread flour, divided
2 tablespoons melted butter, as needed
2 tablespoons granulated sugar, for sprinkling

Preheat the oven to 350 degrees F.

In a mixer with the dough hook attachment, stir together the yeast and warm water. Mix in the milk, sugar, vegetable shortening, salt, eggs, orange extract, orange peel, and half of the flour. Gradually mix in the remaining flour. At medium speed, knead until the dough is smooth and elastic.

Place the dough on a lightly floured surface, cover, and let it rise until it is doubled in size, about 1 to 1 1/2 hours, depending on room temperature—the dough should be in a warm place.

Reshape and form the dough into two large, 10-ounce balls, setting enough dough aside for eight 1-ounce pieces that will form the top 3 "bones" that criss-cross the loaf, and the 1 round ball in the center of each loaf. Place the two round dough balls on a greased cookie sheet, with enough space to allow for rising. Brush the tops lightly with melted butter. Shape the "bones" by rolling out the smaller dough pieces, and crisscross the dough round with them. Finally, place the small round ball in the center of each loaf.

Cover and let the dough rise 45 minutes to 1 hour, or until it has doubled in size. Take care not to let it rise too much or the decorative "bones" will spread out too much during baking.

Bake for about 30 minutes, or until the bottom of the bread is lightly golden brown. Once it has cooled, brush each loaf lightly with melted butter. Let it dry a little, then sprinkle generously with granulated sugar.

*Panifico makes sure to take care of its customers on special occasions—like Dia de Los Muertos. This Mayan and Aztec holiday, which was also influenced by the Catholic faith after the conquistadors arrived in Mexico, celebrates the memory of family and friends who have passed on. On November 1 and 2, the family and friends of the deceased gather at their graveside and bring the loved one's favorite food and drink. No Mexican table would be without the traditional Pan de Muerto around this feast day. This is a recipe that the kids will enjoy making with you!*

## PANIFICO BAKE SHOP
# MEXICAN WEDDING COOKIES

### YIELDS 3 DOZEN (2-INCH) COOKIES

1 cup unsalted butter, room temperature
1/2 cup granulated sugar
1/4 cup powdered sugar, sifted, plus more for dusting
1 tablespoon Mexican vanilla (found in Latin section of grocery or specialty food shops)
1/4 cup (1 or 2) eggs

1 tablespoon baking powder
3/4 teaspoon salt
2 1/2 cups, plus 2 tablespoons all-purpose flour
1/4 cup pecans, finely chopped

Preheat the oven to 375 degrees F. Line 2 cookie sheets with parchment paper.

Using an electric mixer with the paddle attachment, cream the butter and sugars at low speed. Beat in the vanilla and eggs, and mix until smooth. In a separate bowl, sift together the baking powder, salt, and flour. Gradually add this dry mix to the mixer and combine at low speed. Add the pecans, and mix until just blended.

Divide the dough into 1/2-ounce pieces (approximately 1 tablespoon) and shape into balls or crescent shapes. Flatten the balls a bit with your palms to form a traditional cookie shape. Place the dough on cookie sheets, spread evenly apart. Bake for 15 minutes, or until the cookies are lightly browned around the edges. Let them cool, then dust the cookies generously with additional powdered sugar.

*Cookies are universally enjoyed by both children and adults as a quick dessert treat; however, in some instances cookies take an even more important role on the table than simply delighting our tastebuds. Arriving in the United States in the 1950s, Mexican Wedding Cookies have become a beloved Christmastime tradition for many Americans, though they were originally served at Spanish weddings to bestow peace and blessings on the bride and groom. Bakery owner Edna Miggins says that these cookies are great for dunking in coffee—instead of putting sugar in your brew. We agree.*

*Mi Tierra's lively bakery, complete with strolling mariachi singers, is a true dining or shopping experience.*

# CANDIES,
# ICE CREAM, & ICES

Necessity may be the reason for the popularity of iced desserts and other liquid refreshments in San Antonio, which is, after all, a tropical "country." Sometimes it's just too darn hot to consume any other kind of dessert. So, around the month of June, pushcarts and stands topped with umbrellas start appearing around the city—and it's at these oases that a person can choose from a mouthwatering array of flavored ice treats. San Antonions also know that they don't have to wait for the carts to appear: at Fruteria Las Güeras, raspas and frescas are always on the menu. Watermelon, cantaloupe, strawberries, and grapes are just some of the healthy and tasty options for an ice-cold dessert.

Candies have a long history: The Mayans were the first to harvest peanuts, and the Aztecs were big admirers of the vanilla flavor derived from vanilla orchids. Enterprising cooks took advantage (and still do) of a simple candying process, to make little portable treats out of just about any kind of fruit or vegetable. Sweet potatoes, pecans, oranges, lemons, grapefruit, watermelon rinds, cherries, and ginger are great ingredients for surprisingly sophisticated desserts. Mi Tierra Café y Panadería boasts a colorful and extensive selection of candies, so pretty that you almost—but not quite!—hate to eat them.

# Mi Tierra Café y Panadería
# Pecan Praline

### YIELDS 2 DOZEN

2 gallons water
5 pounds granulated sugar
2 ounces butter
1 ounce Mexican vanilla
2 pounds pecan pieces

*If you ever find yourself in San Antonio with a craving for a sweet treat at 3 a.m., your first thought should be Mi Tierra Café y Panadería. Known for its 24-hour "We Never Close" motto and its fabulously eclectic Mexican décor, Mi Tierra Café is a San Antonio institution. Opened by Pete and Cruz Cortez in 1941 as a three-table café for early-rising farmers and workers at San Antonio's old Mercado, this bustling place hasn't seen a dull moment since. Mi Tierra continues to be run by the children and grandchildren of Mr. and Mrs. Cortez as well as long-time employees—like the baker who has been with the restaurant since the bakery opened in 1957. Part of a Mi Tierra tradition, strolling musicians called "los trovadores" may stop at your table to serenade you as you munch on some of the bakery's fabulous, traditional Mexican candies.*

To make the praline syrup, boil water and granulated sugar over high heat for 1 1/2 to 2 hours, or until the syrup thickens. Add the butter, vanilla, and pecans, and stir continuously until the mixture thickens. Spoon the praline mixture in 2- to 3-inch rounds onto a sheet pan lined with wax paper and let them cool for 30 minutes before serving.

NOTE: you can use leftover syrup from pumpkin candies in place of the syrup water. If you do, use 1/2 gallon of the syrup water from the pumpkin candy recipe and only 2 pounds of sugar.

# MI TIERRA CAFÉ Y PANADERÍA
# DULCE DE CALABAZA
# (PUMPKIN CANDY)

## YIELDS 20 TO 40 CANDIES

8 to 10 pounds whole calabaza de castilla, or
  1 large ripe pumpkin
4 1/2 gallons water, divided
5 ounces pickling lime (see note below)
8 pounds granulated sugar, divided

Using a sharp knife, cut the pumpkin meat into uniform wedges or slices, and remove the rind and seeds.

Add 1 1/2 gallons of water to a large stockpot and stir in the lime, making sure that you do not touch the pickling lime with your hands until it has completely dissolved. Using tongs or a slotted spoon, add the pumpkin wedges to the water and lime. The water should cover the pumpkin wedges completely. Soak for 2 to 4 hours—do not soak longer than 4 hours. Drain the pumpkin and rinse it 3 times, very thoroughly, under running water.

Bring another 1 1/2 gallons of water to a boil and add the pumpkin. Boil until the pumpkin wedges are tender, then allow the pumpkin to drain in a colander for about an hour. Pierce each pumpkin wedge with a fork to allow the sugar to penetrate.

To make the syrup, bring another 1 1/2 gallons of water and 4 pounds of granulated sugar to boil. Add the pumpkin and boil for 30 minutes, making sure that the pumpkin doesn't overcook and fall apart. Place the pumpkin on racks over a shallow pan and allow the pumpkin to drain for 24 hours. Save the drained water and cover, as it will be used to repeat the process the following day.

The next day, add another 4 pounds of granulated sugar to the drained pumpkin water from the previous day and add the pumpkin pieces. Bring to a boil, and continue boiling for 30 minutes or until the pumpkin looks shiny, meaning the sugar has crystallized. Drain the pumpkin candy and place on wax paper to dry. Serve warm or cold.

NOTE: Pickling lime, or calcium hydroxide, is a powerful preservative used in canning and pickling to keep vegetables crisp. In Mexico this product is called "Cal" and can be found in specialty grocery stores, garden centers, or hardware stores. Mrs. Wages Lime Powder is the most easily available pickling lime product in the U.S., and can be purchased in Mexican markets, grocery, and hardware stores that sell canning supplies—and also online at www.canningpantry.com/pickling. Use protective gloves and wear long sleeves when handling pickling lime and be careful not to get the lime into your eyes.

*This candy takes two days to make properly but it is well worth it to experience authentic Mexican candy. Mi Tierra is a one-stop shop for everything Mexican; from Mexican hot chocolate to traditional fare for breakfast, lunch, and dinner, to fried ice cream and traditional Mexican bakery items for dessert. You can choose any one of the nine dining rooms that make up this huge restaurant, which is conveniently located in San Antonio's historic Market Square.*

# MI TIERRA CAFÉ Y PANADERÍA
# BANDERILLA DE COCO
# (COCONUT CANDY BARS)

## YIELDS 20 LARGE CANDIES

1/2 gallon water
1 ounce Mexican vanilla
2 ounces butter
2 pounds granulated sugar

1 1/4 pounds coconut flakes
1 bottle green food coloring, as needed
1 bottle red food coloring, as needed

In a large pot, add the water, vanilla, butter, and sugar. Bring the mixture to a boil and continue to cook until it becomes syrupy. Remove from the heat and separate the mixture evenly into three containers.

In the first container of syrup, fold in 1/2 pound of the coconut flakes. Stir in the green food coloring as desired and spread the mixture on an aluminum pan lined with wax paper.

In the second container, fold in 1/2 pound of the coconut flakes. Spread this white mixture over the green coconut.

Repeat the process for the third container, but add the red food coloring to achieve your desire color. Spread the red mixture over the white mixture. Set the pan aside and let it cool for at least 2 hours. Cut coconut candy into long, thin bars, or as desired.

*The most flamboyant establishments in Mexico are the panaderias, or bakeries, with their breads, rolls, cakes, candies, and cookies elaborately decorated in a rainbow of colors, many of them sprinkled with sugar and sporting a rainbow of sugar paste toppings. Every large city in Mexico has several panaderias and even small villages generally have at least one. They are a feast for the eyes as well as the tastebuds!*

# Fruteria Las Güeras
# Agua Fresca (Watermelon, Pineapple, or Cantaloupe)

*Owned and operated by the Ruiz family, Fruteria Las Güeras is a charming outdoor cafe nestled in Northwest San Antonio. It offers a family-friendly spot for the community to enjoy traditional treats of all kinds, including raspas—a San Antonio favorite similar to a snowcone. Philip Ruiz is particularly proud of his agua fresca, which is made with fresh fruit and filtered water, and is a refreshing drink that will lighten the weight of even San Antonio's most oppressive summer days. The enchanting garden-like setting serves as a colorful playground for children as well as a comfortable picnic patio. Frutera Las Güeras received the "Beautify San Antonio Award" from the Beautify San Antonio Association, and is the perfect place to kick back and catch up with friends, family and neighbors—with a cold treat, of course.*

## SERVES 4

1 small seedless watermelon, or large
   pineapple, crushed, juices saved, or
   2 cantaloupes, crushed, and juices saved
1 gallon water
1 1/2 cups granulated sugar (or 1 1/2 cups
   sugar substitute, adjusted to taste)

Select ripe fruit, wash and remove the skins and discard the seeds. In a large mixing bowl, dice and lightly crush the fruit.

Dissolve 1 1/2 cups granulated sugar or sugar substitute into 1 gallon of warm water and slowly mix in the crushed fruit and the natural juices extracted during the crushing process. Chill the beverage with crushed ice or place in the refrigerator for 1 to 2 hours. The frescas keep fresh in the refrigerator for up to two days.

# Don Strange of Texas, Inc.
# Café Mystique

### SERVES 4

1 1/3 cups crushed ice
1 1/3 cups cold espresso, or strong coffee
1 1/3 cups Kahlua liqueur
1/2 cup carnation powdered malt mix

Whipped cream, optional garnish

   Combine all ingredients together in a blender and process until smooth. Serve chilled in tall glasses.

# Ernesto's Restaurant
# Pineapple  Sherbet

### SERVES 4

1 fresh pineapple, sliced
1 pint pineapple sherbet
4 tablespoons Kirschwasser pineapple liqueur
Candied cherries

   Place three scoops each of pineapple sherbet into serving bowls and arrange fresh pineapple slices around. Drizzle pineapple liqueur over sherbet as desired and garnish with a cherry.

# ERNESTO'S RESTAURANT
# CINNAMON ICE CREAM

**SERVES 8**

ICE CREAM
1 cup sugar
1/2 cup half-and-half
1 teaspoon vanilla extract
1 vanilla bean, cut in half lengthwise
2 eggs, beaten
1/2 cup heavy cream
2 teaspoons ground cinnamon

GARNISH
2 tablespoons chopped pecans
2 tablespoons cajeta sauce (found in Latin
    section of grocery, or see recipe, p.53)

To make the ice cream, mix the sugar, half-and-half, vanilla extract, and vanilla bean in a saucepan over low heat. When mixture begins to simmer, but not boil, remove from the heat and allow to rest for 10 minutes. Remove the vanilla bean halves. Over a double boiler, whisk the eggs and add the cream mixture slowly so the eggs do not scramble. Pour the mixture back into the saucepan and add the heavy cream. Cook over medium-low heat for 5 to 8 minutes, stirring constantly, until the mixture is thick enough to coat the back of a spoon. Remove from the heat and whisk in the cinnamon. Set aside to cool. Once cooled, place the mixture into an ice cream maker or freezer until it sets.

Garnish with cajeta sauce and chopped pecans.

# COCO CHOCOLATE LOUNGE & BISTRO
# WHITE CHOCOLATE DISC

4 ounces white chocolate
4 ounces cocoa butter

Melt the white chocolate in a small saucepan over medium-low heat. To construct a white chocolate disc, pour tempered white chocolate onto a sheet of acetate (available at cake and bakery shops), and allow the chocolate to set for 45 minutes to 1 hour, or until it is cool and firm. Remove the acetate and break or cut the chocolate into pieces according to your desired shape.

NOTE: You may want to use a mold to make a perfect chocolate disc or other shape, but you may also pour a free-form circle, or any shape you like onto the acetate. Use your creativity and have fun!

# Index